# Revive and Thrive

## Transforming Parishes into Mission-Driven Communities

Pierre-Alain Giffard

Paulist Press
New York / Mahwah NJ

"Embarking on a transformative journey through the pages of *Revive and Thrive*, Dr. Pierre-Alain Giffard offers a compelling vision for turning parishes into vibrant evangelizing communities. From self-reflection questions that ignite passion to actionable steps for fostering community renewal, this book provides insightful guidance for pastors and church communities alike. An inspiring read for those seeking to navigate the challenges of parish life in a post-2020 world."

**Fr. Michael White**
Co-author of *Rebuilt*

"Comprehensive, compact, concise and compelling, this short book covers it all."

**Fr. James Mallon**
Author of *Divine Renovation*

"What an excellent book… full of key insights and practical suggestions on how to transform parishes into mission-driven communities. Written in a very clear and succinct manner, this book is an excellent *vade mecum* for pastors and parish leaders, especially those parishes struggling with decline. Kudos!"

**Fr. Paul Nwaeze**
Pastor of Holy Redeemer Parish, Ottawa

"In *Revive and Thrive*, Dr. Giffard presents a comprehensive, step-by-step guide for the revitalization of parishes. Confronting the common challenges that parishes often encounter, the book not only instills hope but also provides a plan for breathing new life into the parish community. Each chapter imparts valuable insights and prompts reflection on how change can be ushered in when parishes and parishioners embrace the imperative to fulfill Jesus' Great Commission: 'to go and make disciples.'

Pastors and parishioners in search of revitalization will discover in this book precious resources and a roadmap for navigating the transformative journey, steering their parishes toward becoming mission-driven communities."

**Fr. Paul Shepherd**
Pastor of St. Patrick Parish, Fallowfield

"The parts of the world that used to be called Christendom are now mission territory. There is a new consciousness of the fact that Christian communities must not simply care for the faithful but also, and especially, introduce people to Jesus Christ. But how? How do we move from maintenance to mission, not only in our mentality but also in our methods? Dr. Pierre-Alain Giffard provides parishes and congregations with a step-by-step process that helps Christian communities move from where they are to where they ought to be. Dr. Giffard is to be commended for this important work."

**Fr. Michael Smith**
Pastor of St-Pierre Parish, Fort-Coulonge
Member of the Diocesan Evangelization Team

"I thoroughly enjoyed reading this book and found it to be incredibly powerful and practical. It has called me to re-evaluate the role I play in my own parish. Thank you, Dr. Giffard, for this gift. This powerful and engaging book provides a roadmap for all of us to follow, enabling us to 'love' more individuals back into our parishes and, by extension, our Catholic schools. I wholeheartedly agree: 'With God's grace, any parish can transition to an evangelizing community where seekers are loved into God's Kingdom.'"

**Mark Searson**
Director of Education
Renfrew County Catholic District School Board

And day by day the Lord added to
their number those who were being saved.

Acts 2:47


Cover design: Sandy Lampron
Cover image: Shutterstock / Creative Hawk
Layout: Audrey Wells

Published by Novalis

Publishing Office
1 Eglinton Avenue East, Suite 800
Toronto, Ontario, Canada
M4P 3A1

Head Office
4475 Frontenac Street
Montréal, Québec, Canada
H2H 2S2

en.novalis.ca

Library of Congress Control Number: 2024947463

ISBN 987-0-8091-5754-9 (paperback)
ISBN 978-0-8091-8921-2 (ebook)

Published in the United States by Paulist Press
997 Macarthur Boulevard
Mahwah, New Jersey 07430
www.paulistpress.com

Printed in Canada

# Contents

# Foreword

Over the last eleven years, since my ordination to the episcopacy, I have been a witness to an ever-changing Church that understands, for the most part, an urgent need to focus on its true nature and mission as it faces great challenges in a secular culture. Much has been written and spoken about the call to New Evangelization within our parish communities – and I am truly grateful for that. I have personally insisted on our need to intentionally become a missional Church and continue to support efforts for parish revitalization.

The greatest struggle I have experienced is how to implement the knowledge of the New Evangelization into practical and meaningful ways in our parishes. Too many seem to be stuck in the transition between two models. I believe this book by Dr. Giffard is an excellent proposal for transforming our parishes into mission-driven communities.

The author provides clear and concise theological principles and foundations needed to understand the matter at hand. His pastoral experience out in the field gives him a valuable appreciation of the reality lived in parishes, both urban and rural. This is evident in the questions he provides at the end of every chapter to guide the parish team in integrating the content but also in assessing their own parish reality, potential and challenges. The elements for building a plan of action are all there, no matter where the parish finds itself on this journey in becoming a missionary Church and living it to the fullest.

With the desire for deep conversion and the spiritual renewal of our parish communities, I pray that this reading will inspire many faithful who long to experience a new Pentecost and who seek to proclaim in new ways that Christ Jesus is Saviour and Lord!

*+Marcel Damphousse, Archbishop of Ottawa-Cornwall*

# Introduction

The mission of the Church given by Jesus Christ remains unchanged: "Go therefore and make disciples of all nations, baptizing them in the name of the Father and of the Son and of the Holy Spirit, teaching them to obey everything that I have commanded you" (Matthew 28:19-20). As Catholics, we are called to spread the Gospel and invite others into the life of faith.

Yet, today, many Catholics do not share their faith. Many parishes are grappling with a decline, contending with various challenges in a rapidly changing culture. There is an urgent need to reignite the missionary fire that characterized the early Church and other great periods of the Church. This will require returning to the foundations of disciple-making that still prove effective when embraced.

The purpose of this book is to equip parishes to carry out their mission to make disciples. It offers key insights and practical tips for revitalizing and transforming parish communities. It shows how to create a seamless discipleship pathway and provides guidance for bringing new life and growth to parishes.

We begin by exploring the indispensable role of prayer in empowering and supporting the work of evangelization and parish revitalization. Intercession prepares receptive hearts to receive the Gospel. Building relationships, helping others and sharing our faith stories with those in our sphere of influence are also vital.

An outline for clearly explaining the Good News in compelling ways is shared, aiming to elicit life commitment to following Jesus Christ. We also examine how to create church experiences that effectively welcome and engage secular seekers.

Additionally, we discuss evaluating ourselves from an outsider's perspective and the shifts in vision, culture, focus and leadership required to catalyze an outward, missionary orientation in parishes. This book shares common factors enabling parishes to reinvent themselves as missionary communities.

When using this book in a parish context and group setting to reflect on the needed pastoral changes for a missional shift, maintaining an encouraging and affirming tone is recommended. Recognizing and highlighting the existing good and holy aspects of a parish is essential in fostering a positive and receptive mindset among its members. Every parish, regardless of its size or perceived challenges, has unique strengths and a history of grace-filled moments that have nourished its community. Creating an atmosphere of hope and possibility can inspire individuals to see themselves as active participants in the growth and transformation of their community.

With God's grace, any parish can transition to an evangelizing community where seekers are loved into God's Kingdom. The fields before us stand ripe for harvest. Jesus said to his disciples, "I chose you. And I appointed you to go and bear fruit" (John 15:16). We have been entrusted with this divine mission. May the following chapters reignite our missionary calling as Catholics, equipping our parishes to proclaim the Gospel to all those in need of God's love and mercy.

# 1

# Made to Proclaim

## Recapturing Our Essence as an Evangelizing Church

"As the Father has sent me, so I send you."

—John 20:21

Evangelization lies at the very core of the Church's identity and mission. As Pope Paul VI declared, "Evangelizing is in fact the grace and vocation proper to the Church, her deepest identity. She exists in order to evangelize" (*Evangelii Nuntiandi* §14). This means that the essential purpose and raison d'être of the Church is to spread the Good News of salvation in Jesus Christ and to invite people to become his disciples. Evangelization is not just one ministry among many that the Church does; rather, it encapsulates her entire mission and defines her very nature.

What exactly is evangelization? Pope Paul VI describes it beautifully: "For the Church, evangelizing means bringing the Good News into all the strata of humanity, and through its influence transforming humanity from within and making it new" (*Evangelii Nuntiandi* §18). Essentially, evangelization is about proclaiming the Gospel message in a way that penetrates hearts, transforms lives from the inside out, and leads people into a life-giving relationship with the living God through Jesus Christ.

This mandate to evangelize comes directly from Jesus himself. In the Great Commission recorded in Matthew 28, Jesus instructs his followers,

"Go therefore and make disciples of all nations, baptizing them in the name of the Father and of the Son and of the Holy Spirit, teaching them to obey everything that I have commanded you." He commands them to go out, share the Gospel widely, invite people to become his disciples through baptism and teach them to live according to God's ways. The early Church embraced this calling wholeheartedly, spreading the message of salvation to both Jews and Gentiles. This was no easy task in the face of persecution, and yet, empowered by the Holy Spirit, they faithfully carried out their mission.

As the *Catechism of the Catholic Church* states, "The Church on earth is by her nature missionary" (CCC §850). All of the Church's activities should flow from and be directed toward her evangelizing mission. Her worship, homilies, catechesis, works of charity, faith formation and every other endeavour exist to serve the overarching purpose of bringing Christ to the world. Evangelization gives the Church her vitality; it is her purpose.

Likewise, Pope John Paul II calls for all followers of Christ to be unconditionally evangelizers and witnesses (see *Redemptoris Missio* §45). Every Catholic is called to participate in this mission. For individual believers, evangelization means developing a heart that longs for others to know and love Christ, courageously sharing one's faith and inviting others into friendship with him. For parishes, it means assessing how well their various programs and ministries are geared toward outreach and incorporation of new members. For Church hierarchies, it means evaluating whether their priorities, plans and allocation of resources reflect a commitment to reach the unchurched.

Evangelization requires change and movement. Like the first disciples, we are beckoned to leave our comfort zones and go out to where people are – to the margins – bringing the light of Christ. This means eventually reformatting our parish activities to be more welcoming to newcomers, venturing into our surrounding neighbourhoods to serve the needy, or striking up a conversation about faith with a friend or neighbour. We are called to employ creativity, wisdom and zeal to share the Gospel in ways that resonate with the modern world.

For Catholics and parishes to recover their passion and purpose, evangelization must take centre stage and lead the way. When centred on mission, the Church taps into the very dynamic that Christ intended her to have. She lives out her essence, her identity, her reason for being. May we respond wholeheartedly to Christ's call to evangelize and make disciples, faithfully stewarding the mission he has entrusted to us.

*

Below are some questions aimed at applying the insights gained in this chapter to your personal life or your parish community.

1. How does the Church define evangelization?
2. Why is evangelization considered the core mission of the Church?
3. Why is evangelization seen as a mandate directly from Jesus himself?
4. How does the Great Commission in Matthew 28 guide the Church's mission?
5. In what ways should parish activities flow from and be directed toward its evangelizing mission?
6. How does Pope John Paul II emphasize the role of every Catholic?
7. What does this mean for individual believers, parishes and Church hierarchies?
8. What are the potential benefits of making evangelization a central priority?
9. Does my parish have a deep sense of purpose and passion for sharing the Gospel and making disciples?

I invite you to explore the remaining chapters of the book to kindle your enthusiasm for evangelization and acquire hands-on approaches for fostering a more mission-oriented parish. This guide offers a wealth of insights and resources to help churches recapture their evangelistic zeal and become more effective in reaching out to those who have not yet encountered Jesus Christ and to those who have drifted away from their faith and the Church.

2

# When Prayers Ascend, Power Descends

## Seeking the Spirit to Advance the Kingdom

We exhort all evangelizers, whoever they may be, to pray without ceasing to the Holy Spirit with faith and fervor and to let themselves prudently be guided by Him as the decisive inspirer of their plans, their initiatives and their evangelizing activity.

—Pope Paul VI, *Evangelii Nuntiandi*, §75

Throughout history, the growth of the Church has depended on the Holy Spirit working in response to fervent prayer. Scripture and Church tradition reveal that prayer is the indispensable power source behind advancing the Gospel and bringing people to Christ.

First and foremost, prayer is essential because the conversion of hearts is ultimately God's work, not ours. Jesus himself declared that "No one can come to me unless drawn by the Father who sent me" (John 6:44). It is the Holy Spirit who prompts people to open their lives to Jesus. Our prayers invite the Holy Spirit to move in people's hearts and make them receptive to the Gospel message. When intercessors pray persistently for both the evangelizers and those who will be evangelized, the soil is prepared for seeds to take root.

The Book of Acts provides a vivid example of prayer empowering the Church's evangelizing mission. After Jesus' ascension, the disciples were "constantly devoting themselves to prayer" (Acts 1:14). Shortly after the Holy Spirit descended at Pentecost, Peter preached the Gospel boldly, and 3,000 people were baptized. This astonishing growth came about through the partnership of prayer and proclamation. The disciples' fervent prayers were answered with the Spirit's empowerment, which in turn emboldened them to preach the Gospel with tremendous impact.

Time and again we see the apostles praying and fasting both before and after their evangelistic endeavours (Acts 4:24-31; 13:2-3; 14:23). They acknowledged their dependence on God and cried out for him to act.

In *Divine Renovation Guidebook*, Rev. James Mallon writes, "As more and more of my parishioners have discovered this essential relationship with the third person of the blessed Trinity, the whole tenor of parish life slowly begins to change. Speaking about the Holy Spirit, and praying to and for the Holy Spirit, becomes more natural ... We seek God's power because without it, we can do nothing."[1] At his parish, prayer is central, and they have seen its fruit in parish growth and renewal.

Other thriving churches likewise testify that earnest prayer preceded their revitalization and expansion. Pastor Tommy Barnett of Phoenix First Assembly of God testified that the remarkable growth of his church began when he started encouraging his assembly to pray. They began holding prayer meetings in homes and set up an intercession gathering every Monday at 6:00 a.m. As the church earnestly prayed and sought God, Barnett recalls, "things started to happen, many people came to Christ."[2]

Beyond empowering the proclamation itself, prayer also changes the hearts of the evangelizers. It fills them with love for those who do not know Christ and with compassion to reach out to them. Consistent prayer shapes us into more zealous and effective witnesses for the Gospel. There is a direct correlation between the desire to share Christ's treasure and the intensity of our love for Jesus.

1 James Mallon, *Divine Renovation: From a Maintenance to a Missional Parish* (Toronto: Novalis, 2014), 189.

2 Tommy Barnett and Jim Cymbala, "Revival Begins with Prayer," *Enrichment Journal* (Fall 1996), 22.

Intercession also builds unity within the Body of Christ as parishioners join together to petition the Lord. Within parish life, prayer to support evangelization can take many different forms: parishioners praying individually for friends and family who are estranged from God; prayer groups interceding for both the parish and the local community; Novenas lifting up evangelization endeavours; Eucharistic Adoration to beseech Christ for the outpouring of the Holy Spirit; the prayer of the faithful during Mass; and so on.

So, to live our call to evangelize, we must continually devote time to prayer both individually and corporately within our parishes. As we persevere in prayer, the Holy Spirit will inspire and empower our words and actions to fulfill the Great Commission of making disciples.

To put it concisely, relying on the Holy Spirit is indispensable for renewal. The Spirit empowers witness, converts hearts, distributes gifts and grows the body of Christ. Vibrant spiritual life and evangelistic fruitfulness demonstrate the Spirit's potential when given freedom and cooperation.

The Holy Spirit is always the agent of revival. We must pray to be filled with the Spirit to see our churches come alive again. As Rick Warren explains in his book *The Purpose Driven Church*, "All of our plans, programs, and procedures are worthless without God's anointing. Psalm 127:1 says, 'Unless the LORD builds the house, its builders labor in vain.' A church cannot be built by human effort alone. We must never forget whose church it is. Jesus said, '*I* will build *my* church' (Matt. 16:18, italics added)."[3]

Yes, the harvest belongs to God. Our task is to pray to the Lord of the harvest to send out labourers (Matthew 9:38). Then we must go with confidence in the Spirit's aid. He will produce fruit through us beyond our natural ability. With the Spirit's help we can say, "I can do all things through Christ who strengthens me" (Philippians 4:13) and we will see our churches revived and our communities transformed for God's glory.

As we conclude this chapter, let us now pray for the spiritual renewal of our parish community:

3 Rick Warren, *The Purpose Driven Church: Every Church Is Big in God's Eyes* (Grand Rapids, MI: Zondervan, 1995), 59.

Heavenly Father,
we come before you with humble hearts,
seeking your guidance and wisdom as we strive to become
a more mission-driven community.
We recognize that without your power and presence, our efforts are in vain.
We ask that you pour out your Holy Spirit upon us,
filling us with a deep sense of passion and purpose for sharing the Gospel
and making disciples.
We pray that you ignite a fire in our hearts,
a fire that cannot be quenched,
a fire that will spread throughout our community and beyond.
We ask that you use us as instruments of your grace and mercy,
that we may be effective witnesses for your Kingdom.
Lord, we pray for the spiritual renewal of our community.
If there are walls dividing us, let them fall;
let wounds be mended and our unity be established through your love.
We pray that you raise up leaders who are passionate about your mission,
who are willing to take risks,
and who are committed to making a difference in the world.
We thank you for the privilege of being called to be your ambassadors
and ask all these things in the name of Jesus Christ, our Lord and Saviour.
Amen.

*

Below are some questions aimed at applying the insights gained in this chapter to your personal life or your parish community.

1. How does prayer play a pivotal role in the Church's mission of evangelization?
2. In what ways did the early Church in the Book of Acts demonstrate the power of prayer in their evangelistic efforts?
3. How does a parish's emphasis on prayer and its relationship with the Holy Spirit impact the overall tenor of parish life?
4. How does prayer transform the hearts of the evangelizers?
5. What are some specific forms of prayer that could support and enhance evangelization efforts within your parish community?
6. Why is it crucial for individuals and parishes to devote dedicated time to prayer, both individually and corporately?

# 3

# The Power of a Few

## Small Groups Fan the Flames

The power of small groups comes from
forming relationships
in which conversations lead to conversion.

–Rev. Michael White and Tom Corcoran, *Rebuilt*

Small groups *focused on outreach* are consistently identified as a key component of effective evangelization and discipleship within parishes. While large-group gatherings like Sunday Mass are crucial, small groups provide a uniquely fertile soil for seekers to explore faith, build community and grow as followers of Jesus.

### What Is a Small Group?

A small group is a gathering of around three to twelve people who meet regularly for spiritual purposes. Common small-group activities include Bible study, viewing faith-oriented video content, prayer, worship and discussion. Groups are usually led by a lay person and meet in homes, coffee shops or church meeting rooms.

Small groups are effective for several reasons. First, they allow people to build close relationships founded on trust and openness. In a small-group context, newcomers find a safe space to share their lives, ask questions, voice doubts and pray together. The intimacy and accountability of the group accelerates spiritual discovery and growth. Members encourage one another, model Christian life and care for each person like family.

Second, small groups equip people for evangelization. In groups oriented around outreach, members are encouraged to share their personal faith stories with others. Prayer and discussion build their courage and desire to reach out. Their evangelization is relationally based, inviting into the group friends, neighbours and colleagues who already know and trust them.

Third, small groups provide an easy way for newcomers to plug into church life and grow in faith. The familiar setting and relationships give traction for spiritual growth as group members read the Bible, watch videos, pray and discuss applying their faith. For seekers exploring Christianity, a small group provides a comfortable place to process new ideas and ask candid questions.

Fourth, small groups cultivate lay leadership. As participants take turns facilitating discussion or mentoring a new believer, leadership gifts emerge. As groups multiply, new leaders can be raised up and get involved in other parish ministries.

Fifth, small groups promote a sense of fellowship and community. Large parish gatherings can easily lead to people feeling unnoticed and unwelcome. But it's nearly impossible to go unnoticed in a group of three to twelve people meeting regularly as they form close relationships.

Sixth, small groups can foster the use of spiritual gifts. In a large-group setting, only the most public gifts like teaching or administration are exercised. But in a small group, more private gifts come into play, like encouragement, service, wisdom and exhortation. More people contribute rather than relying on the priest or a handful of leaders.

Seventh, small groups provide pastoral care and support. During times of crisis or loss, a small group surrounds the individual as a spiritual family. Hospital visits, meals, childcare and prayer uplift the one in need. In times of illness, addiction or depression, the group loves the person through the struggle.

Eighth, small groups help new believers and seekers process doubts, questions and objections to faith. In a large setting, it's hard or impossible to voice doubts candidly without disrupting others. But in a group's safe space, doubts can be unpacked and resolved through prayer and digging into Scripture together. Honest questioning in community propels growth.

Ninth, small groups allow diversity in worship and programming appropriate to members' ages and life stages. Groups can gather in homes at convenient times with flexible formats tailored to their needs and interests. The broader church still gathers corporately, but small groups diversify programming.

In summary, small groups focused on outreach, Bible study, care for one another and fellowship provide a great structure for integrating new believers into the Church. Small groups provide the personal soil where faith blooms. They have the potential of transforming newcomers into mature disciples who live out Christianity with love, passion and purpose.

Having said this, it is also important to recognize that small groups are not the exclusive approach to evangelization and discipleship. Some individuals may have social or personal circumstances that make it challenging for them to participate in regular small-group activities. A parish should strive to provide a variety of gathering opportunities that cater to the diverse needs and preferences of its members, ensuring that everyone has the chance to grow in their faith in a way that resonates with them.

Finally, we need to consider two critical points. First, small groups that do not engage those who have not yet encountered Jesus Christ or those who have drifted away from the Church tend to stagnate and diminish over time. It is essential that small groups evangelize. Second, maintaining a close connection with the parish ensures that small groups don't become isolated or deviate from the broader Church.

*

Below are some questions aimed at applying the insights gained in this chapter to your personal life or your parish community.

1. What are the defining characteristics of a small evangelizing group?
2. How do they differ from larger-group gatherings within a parish setting?
3. In what ways can small evangelization groups equip individuals for outreach?
4. How does their approach to evangelization differ from other methods?
5. What role do small evangelization groups play in cultivating lay leadership within the parish?
6. In what ways do small groups allow for the exercise of a wider range of spiritual gifts and encourage greater participation from group members?
7. How can small groups provide pastoral care and support to individuals during times of crisis, loss and personal struggles?

# 4

# Where Outsiders Meet Insiders

## Reframing Ministry Through an Unchurched Lens

Invite a non-parishioner, a fallen-away Catholic, a non-Catholic Christian and a non-Christian to come to your church and report back to you what it was like.

—Fr. James Mallon, *Divine Renovation Guidebook*

For parishes that desire to effectively reach and retain new people, adopting the perspective of the unchurched[4] is essential. Seeing our parish and its programs through the eyes of those unfamiliar with Christianity provides invaluable insight to make our communities more hospitable and our message more understandable.

First, many unchurched people find church culture, vocabulary and unspoken rules confusing and intimidating. Acronyms, theological jargon,[5] uptight etiquette and foreign rituals can engender feelings of discomfort, inadequacy and exclusion. Evaluating these practices and explaining unfamiliar elements, through intentional preaching, for example, can assist in enlightening the unchurched and create a more welcoming environment.

4 Although it has limitations, we will use the term "unchurched" to identify individuals who have not received the Gospel, seekers or disengaged Catholics.

5 Many words in the Catholic faith are incomprehensible to the unchurched, and even to some Catholics, such as justification, Triduum, Trinity, transubstantiation, grace, magisterium and the lectionary, to name a few.

Second, newcomers often struggle to follow the flow of worship services. Following along in hymnals, standing, kneeling and sitting at certain times feels awkward. Unclear signage and directions to facilities like nurseries or restrooms causes frustration. Examining the service's logical flow through an outsider's eyes reveals simple improvements to smooth out their experience.

Third, unchurched people also may perceive homilies as irrelevant, impersonal and disconnected from real life. Preaching that connects Scripture and theology to contemporary issues in down-to-earth language makes the message's relevance click. Personal illustrations also foster engagement. Messages should aim to ignite interest and a response to the Gospel, not just communicate information.

Fourth, unchurched visitors quickly determine whether a parish cares about them. Greeters who converse personally and avoid awkwardness foster connection. Follow-up that shows the parish desires a relationship beyond just attendance builds trust. Cultivating authentic care and concern is crucial.

Fifth, the unchurched may harbour objections, doubts or concerns about faith claims. Directly addressing common sticking points such as hypocrisy, suffering, felt exclusion and judgmentalism with them helps break through intellectual barriers. Treating doubts and misconceptions with empathy rather than defensiveness eases worries.

Sixth, unchurched people generally lack understanding of salvation. The logic of Jesus' atoning death reconciling humanity to God often makes little sense. Preaching explaining salvation and extending clear invitations to respond to the Gospel aids comprehension and decision making. Additional classes or sessions can further clarify the meaning and consequences of salvation.

Seventh, outsiders often struggle to grasp the concept of grace. Explaining God's amazing grace, unconditional love and forgiveness through Christ undoes false views of God. Celebrating grace-based conversion stories further cements this truth.

Eighth, unchurched visitors often feel anonymous and overwhelmed by large crowds at first. Small groups, classes and service teams help them make connections. Name tags aid in learning each other's names.

Friendly members who chat and sit with newcomers foster belonging. Intimate community makes big settings more navigable.

Ninth, newcomers may be unaware of available classes, studies, programs and volunteer opportunities for getting involved. Personal conversations, bulletins and announcements should explain options clearly. The parish website and printed guides describing entry points and next steps facilitate engagement. Sign-ups near exits increase commitment.

Evaluating ourselves from the outsider's perspective yields many revelations about how to shape our language, facilities, programming and culture to make it easier and desirable for unchurched people to discover and follow Christ. While maintaining theological depth and worshipful reverence, we should adapt all non-essentials to make our parishes welcoming places for those exploring faith. Just as Jesus drew sinners and outsiders close through healing and compassion, our communities must be safe havens where seeking people meet a God who loves them, heals them and cherishes them.

Imagine walking down the street near your parish building. What first impressions do the grounds and facility give? Is the entrance easy to find? Is the signage clear? Is the lawn well kept? Are there places to sit and relax? A missionary parish needs to consider these questions from a newcomer's perspective, making changes as needed.

Now picture yourself coming to attend a worship service at your parish for the first time. Is parking readily available? Are greeters present to welcome you and show you around? Does the bulletin use understandable terms? Are the hymns easy to sing along to? Is technology used effectively? Do visual elements like art and media engage the senses?

Finally, envision the days following your first visit. Do parish members follow up to say they are glad you came? Are you invited to a small group or next-steps class? Making newcomers feel noticed and cared for increases the likelihood of return visits and eventual commitment.

## Programming for Spiritual Seekers

The unchurched are often spiritual seekers looking for meaning and purpose. Missionary parishes, big and small, design entry points tailored to skeptics. Topical mini-courses on issues like relationships, addiction and parenting help introduce seekers to the Bible's life-giving relevance. Alpha Courses[6] create relaxed environments for people to freely ask questions and discuss faith. Special seeker services present the Gospel message in engaging ways through media and testimonies. Creating services where invitees feel comfortable is key.

## Accessibility

To interest new people, parishes must eliminate barriers. Analyze all aspects of parish life for accessibility: facilities, parking, language, music style, childcare, flow of services, and so on.

Using insider church vocabulary makes visitors feel excluded. Explaining traditions and elements of liturgy is important for the unchurched. Services should be understandable for spiritual seekers still learning the faith. Music styles should vary across traditional and contemporary. Making disciples requires meeting people where they are.

## Authentic Community

Loneliness and disconnection from community plague many today. People crave meaningful relationships. Small groups foster interpersonal bonds and provide conduits for newcomers to experience belonging. Authentic fellowship shows the beauty of the Gospel embodied in loving Christians. Testimonies of life transformation inspire seekers. Missionary parishes don't expect immediate commitment but patiently walk with spiritual pilgrims as relationships grow.

## Meeting Felt Needs

Serving the community addresses real needs and builds bridges for the Gospel. Service projects, addiction support groups, immigration aid and housing assistance meet needs the unchurched may have. People don't care how much we know until they know how much we care. As Christians show God's compassion through practical help, doors open

6 For additional details on Alpha Courses, check out the regional Alpha websites: Canada – alphacanada.org; USA – alpha.org; UK – alpha.org.uk; Australia – alpha.org.au.

for eventually offering spiritual hope. Parishes desiring renewal must look outward and discern how to meet needs around them.

To sum up, placing oneself in the shoes of the unchurched sheds light on how to adapt the way we do church and to create parish experiences that resonate with secular seekers. While certain core elements of worship gatherings will remain, making changes to be sensitive and hospitable to unbelievers is necessary. As Paul said, "I have become all things to all people, so that I might by any means save some" (1 Corinthians 9:22).

*

Below are some questions aimed at applying the insights gained in this chapter to your personal life or your parish community.

1. How can we evaluate our parish practices and celebrations to ensure they are not confusing or intimidating to the unchurched?
2. What improvements can be made to the worship service flow to help newcomers feel more comfortable and engaged?
3. How about the quality of our website? Is it easy to navigate? How easy is it to find Mass times or other information? Is the information up to date?
4. How could we encourage our parish priest to make homilies more relevant, relatable and connected to real-life issues?
5. What steps can we take to demonstrate genuine care and concern for newcomers beyond just their attendance?
6. What can we do to explain the concept of salvation in a way that is clear and understandable to the unchurched?
7. How can we ensure that information about available classes, studies, programs and volunteer opportunities is easily accessible to newcomers?

5

# From Stranger to Friend
## Sharing Christ Along Life's Journey

"Love is the force that opens hearts to the word of Jesus and to his Redemption."

–Saint John Paul II, Mass at Grant Park, Chicago, 1979

Relationships are a crucial component – perhaps the most important component – in evangelization. While programs, events and materials should not be ignored, it is through personal connections that the Gospel spreads most powerfully. Jesus himself modelled relational ministry, sharing God's love as he lived among people.

Statistics show that a majority of people who embrace Christianity do so because of friends or family members who shared Christ with them or invited them to church. Their positive example made the difference. When a friend shares how their faith has shaped their life, unbelieving family and friends are far more open to the message. The existing relationship provides a level of trust and openness that strangers lack. This was how the early Church grew: through friends inviting friends, relatives inviting relatives to consider Christ.

We can think about our own journey. Weren't we introduced to Jesus through people we knew and trusted? Whether it was a parent, sibling, friend, coworker or neighbour, a personal relationship opened the door to faith. Relationships, over time, let people see faith bear fruit in love. When people witness compassion, forgiveness, integrity and service in our lives, it makes the message plausible.

A stranger delivering urgent news on the street may make us skeptical. But if our best friend shares important information, we will likely listen with an open mind because we know and trust them. It's similar with evangelization: relationships enable the message to be heard.

Evangelization through relationships recognizes that people's hearts must be cultivated over time through service, love and repeated encounters with the Gospel message. In the same way that good soil requires plowing, sowing, watering and weeding for fruit to grow, people's hearts are prepared gradually through layers of loving interaction. Just sowing the seed without cultivating relationships leads to little lasting fruit.

Relationships allow us to share faith in ways tailored to an individual's unique personality, questions and needs. Customizing examples to their situation makes the message penetrate their heart uniquely. We listen and discuss together, welcoming objections, doubts and experiences that enrich our spiritual understanding. Evangelization becomes a mutual exchange. By loving, listening, praying, and sharing the Gospel, we simply collaborate with the Holy Spirit's role of implanting faith. We play our part and trust God with the outcome.

Relationship-based evangelization also provides the context of community needed to sustain new believers. When our friend circles embrace a new believer, they find support to withstand trials that might otherwise snuff out their newborn faith. Relationships provide perseverance. Christian fellowship itself attracts people to the Gospel. In a fragmented world, sincere love and welcome draw people together. Some people first visit a church simply seeking community.

Evangelization through relationships enables us to see people not as projects but as precious individuals loved by God. We share faith because we care for them, not to notch another convert. Even if they never embrace Christ, we continue to love them as cherished creations of God. The relationship has intrinsic divine worth beyond "results."

In summary, evangelization was never meant to happen apart from personal connections. Just as Jesus walked with his disciples, taking time to know them, answer their concerns and shape them spiritually, we should follow his relational model. Programs have a place, but only relationships transform lives through the slow work of authentic caring, listening and faith sharing. This form of evangelization does take time, but the lasting spiritual fruit is well worth it. As people open their hearts through relationships, the Gospel changes their lives from the inside out. Our availability, care and persistence allow God to communicate his grace to those around us. Love remains the most convincing apologetic.

Here are some habits that can help us relationally share Christ:

- Praying regularly for specific people we want to reach, asking God to open doors and empower us.
- Showing unconditional love. Treating others as precious in God's eyes. Offering to help with practical needs. Service demonstrates Christ's love.
- Asking good questions. Not interrogating people, but showing interest in their lives, values and beliefs. Listening more than speaking.
- Sharing casually about our spiritual life or things God has taught us. Not keeping our faith private.
- Extending invitations at the right time to appropriate events or small groups, and making sure they know we want them to come.
- Telling our story of conversion. Keeping it concise, authentic and relatable.
- After people come to faith, getting them plugged into a church body quickly. Community nurtures growth.

*

Below are some questions aimed at applying the insights gained in this chapter to your personal life or your parish community.

1. How have personal relationships played a role in my own journey of faith and introduction to Jesus?
2. Why is building trust and openness through relationships important in effective evangelization?
3. How can I cultivate and nurture new relationships with friends, coworkers or neighbours?
4. In what ways can I demonstrate compassion, forgiveness, integrity and service in my life to make the message of faith more plausible to others?
5. How can I create a context of Christian fellowship and community that supports and sustains new believers?
6. What habits can I develop, such as praying, showing unconditional love, asking good questions and sharing my spiritual life, to engage in relational evangelization?
7. How can I actively support and integrate new believers into my parish community to foster growth and discipleship?

# 6

# All Hands on Deck
## Revamping Parish Life for Mission

Be transformed by the renewing of your minds,
so that you may discern what is the will of God
–what is good and acceptable and perfect.
–Romans 12:2

Parishes are called to go out and share the Gospel with others, to make disciples of all nations (Matthew 28:19). This requires adopting a missionary mindset and being willing to change in order to effectively reach those who don't know Christ.

The shift toward being an evangelizing parish is not a matter of chance or an immediate transformation. It involves a thoughtful and incremental process that occurs over time. Below are some pivotal mindsets and shifts that can steer parishes toward a heightened missionary focus.

- *Prioritize the unchurched*: Missionary churches make reaching the unchurched a top priority. They see themselves as mission outposts and feel an urgent need to reach out to those who do not know God's love and mercy. This involves assessing budgets, programs and activities based on how well they attract new individuals to Christ and the Church. Does the parish have any programs for outreach, evangelization and discipleship? Which current activities are effectively reaching out to those who are not regularly attending church? Which ones are not as impactful? Asking these questions with humility is the first step.

- *Modify your leadership style*: Transition to a missionary mode means modifying leadership style and skills. Leaders should demonstrate an ardent evangelistic spirit and empower their followers to do the same. Vision casting, mobilizing change, lay training and team building allow priests and lay leaders to design the shift. Missionary transition surfaces fears that must be overcome. Fear of rejection when implementing changes, fear of members leaving and fear of failure can paralyze leadership. Faith in God's purposes and sensitivity to concerns while still leading are imperative. Mistakes will occur, and some efforts may be abandoned, but leaders cannot lose heart and must stay the course through constant prayer.
- *Prune less-essential ministries*: Missionary transition may require eliminating or pruning less-essential ministries. Limiting activities frees energy and resources for the most critical work of evangelization. Saying no to peripheral activities makes space for the essential.
- *Focus on the weekend experience*: For most unchurched visitors, weekend celebrations will be their first and most important impression of the Church. Therefore, missionary churches pay close attention to the weekend experience, striving to make services engaging, accessible and welcoming to newcomers.
- *Train greeters and ushers*: Those who greet visitors, answer any questions and seat them for worship on busy occasions play a crucial role. Missionary churches invest in training greeters and ushers to be warm, friendly and helpful to newcomers. A smile, a handshake and a short conversation go a long way!
- *Evaluate facilities*: The condition of parish facilities also affects first impressions. Though extensive renovations may not be possible, keeping buildings clean, easy to navigate and well maintained shows visitors that you have created a welcoming space for them.
- *Engage in missionary preaching*: For the unchurched, the homily is often the highlight of their visit. Homilies should aim to connect with and inspire newcomers. Avoid too much insider language and teach

theological and spiritual principles clearly. Proclaim the kerygma, the call of Jesus to conversion.

- *Offer clear next steps*: Missionary churches provide clear next steps for interested visitors, like a newcomers' reception or homily notes. Connecting visitors to a small group is also important. Follow-up is key.
- *Create multiple entry points*: Becoming missionary means expanding avenues for people to begin a faith journey. Classes, small groups and service projects should require no prior church background. Entry points for the unchurched must multiply through warm hospitality efforts and clear website information.
- *Focus on integration*: Integrating newcomers into the church community is crucial.

Missionary churches have systems to help visitors become active members through classes, mentorship programs or joining lay ministry teams.

- *Equip for outreach*: Missionary parishes train members to share their faith. Outreach events like service projects, potluck meals or processions are organized. The more members are directly engaged in evangelization, the more the church will grow.
- *Pray!* Change requires spiritual power. Prayer unleashes God's power. Pastor Warren says, "Of course, prayer *is* absolutely essential. Every step of Saddleback's development has been bathed in prayer. In fact, I have a prayer team that prays for me *while I speak* at each of our four weekend services. A prayerless ministry is a powerless ministry."[7] Churches desiring renewal must devote themselves to united prayer.
- *Change the metrics*: What gets measured gets done. Rather than just counting total attendees, missionary churches track new professions of faith, adult baptisms and newly engaged members. Celebrating changed lives fosters a missionary culture.

---

7 Rick Warren, *The Purpose Driven Church: Every Church Is Big in God's Eyes* (Grand Rapids, MI: Zondervan, 1995), 58.

- *Accept losses*: As parishes transition to a more outward-oriented approach, certain members might decide to leave the community. Although this can be a painful experience, parishes must not be discouraged from embracing missionary renewal due to the objections or departures of a few. Our focus should remain steadfast on reaching out and making new disciples.
- *Recognize that change is difficult*: Transitioning an established parish to become more outwardly focused will not be easy. Change often requires replacing familiar programs and ways of doing things with new initiatives. While preserving the essence of tradition and holding fast to unchanging doctrinal truth, it is equally crucial to recognize that the world and human society are constantly evolving. Parishes must adapt to better connect with today's society. We must adjust in order to bring the Gospel to the communities of today.

In brief, churches desiring missionary renewal must take an honest look at themselves, be open to new methods and programs, and steadfastly make the changes needed to become more outwardly focused on those who don't know Christ. This will take time, prayer and perseverance. With God's help, parishes can make the challenging yet necessary changes to become missionary communities that actively seek to reach the lost with the life-saving message of the Gospel. Some efforts and new outreach experiments will fail, but pastoral innovation is key.

*

Below are some questions aimed at applying the insights gained in this chapter to your personal life or your parish community.

1. How have I personally observed the effects of an inwardly focused parish and its impact on declining membership?
2. In what ways can we prioritize reaching the unchurched and make it a top priority in our own parish?
3. What leadership style modifications and skills would be needed to effectively lead a transition toward a more missionary-focused approach?
4. Which less-essential ministries in our parish might need to be pruned or eliminated to free up resources for evangelization efforts?
5. How can we enhance the weekend experience in my parish to make it engaging, accessible and welcoming to newcomers?
6. What steps can we take to train and equip greeters and ushers to create a warm and friendly environment for visitors?
7. How can we improve the condition of our parish facilities to create positive first impressions for newcomers?
8. What practical next steps can we offer to interested visitors to help them integrate into the church community and engage in discipleship?

# 7

# Pastoral Shepherds of Revival

## The Priest's Role in Catalyzing Renewal

> The priest should give priority to proclaiming the gospel message to those in the area who have not yet been baptized. First evangelization is a basic duty that the Church, through the apostles, has received from the Lord himself: 'Go out to the whole world; proclaim the Good News to all creation' (Mk 16:15; cf. Mt 28:19).
>
> —Congregation for the Evangelization of Peoples, *Pastoral Guide for Diocesan Priests*, §7 (1989)

Priests play a key role in renewing and growing a parish through casting vision, equipping the laity and fostering a missionary culture. Empowered lay leaders are also essential for driving change and engaging the wider community.

### Casting Vision

Priests serve as the primary vision casters and lead communicators in a parish. A compelling vision helps give direction and purpose, motivating parishioners to participate in realizing it. Priests should communicate the missionary vision in an inspirational yet understandable way. The vision ought to challenge the status quo and aim to reach new people with the Gospel. During his homilies, the priest will regularly reiterate and reinforce the vision.

## Equipping the Laity

Rather than doing ministry alone, priests should equip lay leaders. Moses could not judge the Israelites alone and appointed leaders to share the burden (Exodus 18). Priests can share power and responsibility while still retaining authority. Equipping requires instilling vision, mentoring emerging leaders and providing training. Small-group leader formation is essential for growth. Priests should help people identify their spiritual gifts and plug into suitable ministries.

## Fostering Missionary Culture

A missionary culture is one oriented outward to reach those who don't know Jesus. As the primary leader, the priest must model evangelistic living and continually foster a missionary ethos through preaching, vision casting and programming. The priest is the "missionary-in-chief" and is passionate about reaching the lost. Dedicated prayer for revitalization and evangelization is critical for the priest personally and to be promoted among the faithful.

## Engaging the Community

Priests should ensure the church engages the community outside its walls through needs-focused ministries and special outreach events. They can spearhead compassion initiatives like free meals for those in need, addiction support groups or immigration services. Outreach events like potlucks, pilgrimages, processions and holiday celebrations open doors to invite neighbours. The priest should model casual evangelization in community spaces.

## Lay Leadership Development

Empowering lay leaders is crucial for long-term growth and the priest's mental and physical well-being. Exodus 18 shows that God never intended for one leader to shoulder all ministry responsibilities alone. Priests should identify and equip natural leaders from the parish to oversee lay ministries. Letting go of control while providing mentoring creates shared ownership. Leaders can be developed through hands-on ministry experience coupled with coaching and formal training. Leadership pipelines ensure that new leaders rise up.

## Developing an Evangelizing Spirituality

Priests must foster an evangelizing spirituality among parishioners rooted in an intimate relationship with Christ, cultivating love for God, our neighbours and making disciples. Regular Scripture reading and reception of sacraments open our hearts to God's desires: that all may know God and find life in Jesus through the Holy Spirit. This spirituality ignites the passion to share God's transformative love with others. As parishioners grow closer to God's desire for all to be saved, their hearts grow in compassion to reach others.

## Driving Change

Implementing changes to become more outwardly focused requires determination and perseverance. Change often faces resistance. Priests must remain anchored to the vision and the "why" behind the proposed missionary changes. Patience and engaging communication are key to reassuring concerned parishioners. Change is a process that takes time. Progress may seem slow, but pressing forward with small steps of improvement leads to a transformed parish over the long term.

In summary, priests have a central role in catalyzing renewal and evangelization through missionary governance, preaching, sanctifying, training and community engagement. Their preaching contextualizes the Gospel message and Catholic teachings in ways that connect with the unchurched. Pastoral leadership involves guiding parishioners to live as missionary disciples who share their faith. By overseeing outreach ministries and creating a welcoming culture, priests help the parish orient outward. They model evangelistic living through their own examples of relational evangelization. Everything the priests do as sacramental ministers, preachers and shepherds aims to draw people into a life-giving relationship with Jesus Christ and his Church. In their three-fold ministry, priests are configured to Christ the Evangelizer, who came to seek and save the lost.

While delegating and empowering lay leaders, priests must also demonstrate tireless commitment to Church revitalization. They should themselves be evangelistic models who openly share their faith, invite new people to church and cultivate spiritual conversations. Their example gives parishioners courage to do likewise. With God-fuelled conviction, creativity and consistent effort by both priests and laity, parishes can reach their full evangelistic potential.

*

Below are some questions for priests aimed at applying the insights gained in this chapter.

1. How can I, as a priest, effectively communicate a vision for evangelization that motivates and inspires parishioners?
2. How can I foster a missionary culture in my parish that directs its focus outward to reach those who don't know Jesus?
3. What specific outreach initiatives and community engagement strategies can be implemented to ensure that my parish is actively engaging with the needs of the community outside its walls?
4. How can I identify and develop natural leaders within my parish who can oversee and lead lay ministries, ensuring shared ownership and long-term growth?
5. What practices and spiritual disciplines can I encourage among parishioners to cultivate an evangelizing spirituality rooted in an intimate relationship with Christ?

6. How can I effectively navigate and manage resistance to change that may arise when implementing missionary-focused initiatives in my parish?
7. What steps can I take to ensure that my preaching effectively connects with the unchurched, contextualizing the Gospel message and Catholic teachings in ways that resonate with them?
8. How can I create a welcoming culture within my parish that encourages parishioners to invite others and engage in spiritual friendship?
9. What practical actions can I personally take to be an evangelization model, openly sharing my faith, inviting new people to church and cultivating spiritual conversations?

# 8

# Connecting the Dots
## Creating Seamless Discipleship Pathways

Part of an effective evangelism process is leading people who visit to become disciples and, eventually, leaders. That process includes welcoming guests, connecting people, assimilating new believers, and discipling members.

—Ed Stetzer and Mike Dodson, Comeback Churches

For a parish to carry out its core mission, it needs a clear process for evangelizing and guiding people to become disciples of Jesus Christ. This chapter outlines such a process and practical steps to implement it.

### The Discipleship Process

The Oxford dictionary defines a process as "a series of actions or steps taken in order to achieve a particular end." A discipleship process consists of an interrelated series of pastoral activities that engage new people with the Gospel and lead them from a state of indifference or distrust toward the Church to an initial encounter with Christ, and then to a commitment and service within the Church and in the world.

At each stage of the process, parishioners accompany the evangelized to the next step of their journey. The process equips the parish to carry out Jesus' commission to "go and make disciples of all nations" (Matthew 28:19). It provides a path through the following stages:

1. *Evangelization* (missionary outreach): Parishioners actively reach out to those who have not yet chosen to follow Christ to share the Gospel message through service, personal invitations, small groups and events offering an experience of Christian community.
2. *Welcoming*: Greeters, ushers and hospitality teams ensure that visitors and new attendees feel warmly welcomed and cared for at weekend liturgies and parish events. Follow-up contacts are made.
3. *Sacramental initiation*: Inquiry classes and the Rite of Christian Initiation of Adults (RCIA) prepare new believers for baptism and full initiation into the Church.
4. *Integration*: New members are drawn into parish life through mentorships with other parishioners, serving in lay ministries, joining small faith-sharing groups and making friends.
5. *Spiritual growth*: Ongoing catechesis through Bible studies, adult faith formation, retreats and small groups fosters continuing growth in understanding of the faith and developing a relationship with Christ.
6. *Missionary discipleship*: Formed disciples discern how to use their spiritual gifts. Leadership development prepares them to share in the parish's mission.

## How can a parish implement such a discipleship process?

- *Identify gaps*: Assess current ministries and programs against the six stages of the process to find missing components.
- *Connect ministries*: Get ministry leaders communicating to hand off new members from one stage to the next. Adjustments to programs and ministries will align them with the six stages above. When all parish ministries interlock in this integrated process, new disciples are formed.

## Signs of Progress

How will a parish know its process is bearing fruit? Key signs include:

- Parishioners taking up their role as evangelizers
- New outreach events drawing in the unchurched
- The parish environment feeling welcoming to newcomers
- Seekers participating in inquiry classes and RCIA
- New members joining parish small groups and serving in ministries
- Laity being empowered for ministry through leadership development
- New disciples participating in outreach ministries as missionary parishioners

As evangelization and disciple-making become the focus guiding parish decisions and activities, the Church's evangelizing mission comes alive. New people encounter Christ, and new disciples are made and are empowered to bear fruit of conversion and share the Gospel with others.

*

Below are some questions aimed at applying the insights gained in this chapter to your parish community.

1. How well does my parish currently engage in missionary outreach and actively reach out to those who have not yet chosen to follow Christ?
2. How effective are we in creating a welcoming environment for visitors and new attendees during liturgies and parish events?
3. Are we providing adequate preparation and support for individuals, both adults and children, seeking sacramental initiation?
4. Are we actively integrating new members into parish life and providing opportunities for mentorships, lay ministries and small faith-sharing groups?

5. How well are we nurturing the spiritual growth of our parishioners through ongoing catechesis, Bible studies, adult faith formation, retreats and small groups?
6. Are we effectively fostering missionary discipleship and helping formed disciples discern and utilize their spiritual gifts?
7. How can we enhance our leadership development programs to better prepare individuals to share in the parish's evangelizing mission?
8. What gaps exist in our current ministries and programs when compared to the six stages of the discipleship process? How can we address these gaps to ensure a comprehensive and integrated approach to discipleship?
9. How can we improve communication and collaboration among ministry leaders to facilitate the seamless transition of individuals from one stage of the process to the next?
10. What signs of progress can we look for to gauge the effectiveness of our discipleship process?
11. How will we know if parishioners are actively embracing their role as evangelizers, if outreach events are drawing in the unchurched and if new members are becoming engaged in small groups and ministries?
12. How can we ensure that evangelization and disciple-making become the guiding focus of our parish's decisions and activities?

9

# Built for Mission
## Structuring a Team for Parish Revitalization

Where there is no guidance, a nation falls;
but in an abundance of counsellors there is safety.

—Proverbs 11:14

A dedicated evangelization team is crucial for parish revitalization, as it keeps the Great Commission at the forefront of parish life. It also enables effective planning despite the challenges of a busy parish life.

To form an evangelization team, the first step is to select a diverse group of creative parishioners. This team should consist of individuals willing to think outside the box while providing honest insights about existing problems and opportunities.

The team's size should ideally be between five and eight members to facilitate robust discussions. A commitment to sustained, long-term efforts in parish renewal and rebuilding is essential, with the pastor's support being crucial. It's beneficial to have a lay leader coordinating the team's efforts.

Here are three principles for creating an evangelization team for your parish[8]:

8 See The Malphurs Group, "Building Your Revitalization Team," https://malphursgroup.com/building-your-revitalization-team.

- *Have diverse representation*: Ensure that the team includes a broad cross-section of your parish to avoid relying solely on the board or staff. Involving various members of the faith community provides a comprehensive perspective and prevents leadership fatigue and lack of buy-in.
- *Utilize influential individuals*: Enlist known leaders in your church, both those with official titles and those with influence but no formal position. Having a mix of men and women, representing different age groups and life experiences, adds valuable perspectives.
- *Aim for positivity and constructive criticism*: Select only positive individuals who genuinely care about the Church's well-being and are willing to change, to work hard to achieve positive outcomes. Avoid including people with negative attitudes, the paralyzingly prudent or those who vent frustrations during team discussions.

Look for team members with gifts in areas like outreach, hospitality, communication and planning. It's crucial to have voices from various segments of the parish community, embracing diversity in age, gender, ethnicity and involvement in parish life. Team members who are passionate about evangelization and open to new ideas are ideal candidates.

Before beginning its planning work, the evangelization team must first identify what can revitalize a parish and, whenever possible, visit renewed and growing churches.

*

Below are some questions aimed at applying the insights gained in this chapter to your parish community.

1. What criteria should we consider when selecting individuals for our evangelization team?
2. How can we ensure that the team consists of diverse, creative parishioners who can provide honest insights about existing problems and opportunities?

3. How can we determine the optimal size for our evangelization team?
4. What qualities should we look for in potential team members?
5. How can we identify individuals who possess gifts and talents in areas such as outreach, hospitality, communication and planning?
6. What factors should we consider to facilitate robust discussions and efficient decision-making processes?
7. Do we have a clear commitment from team members to engage in sustained, long-term efforts for parish renewal and rebuilding?
8. How can we foster a sense of dedication and perseverance within the team?
9. What role should the pastor play in supporting the evangelization team?
10. How can we ensure that the pastor's involvement and endorsement are integral to the team's efforts?
11. What are the benefits of having a lay leader coordinate the evangelization team's efforts?
12. How can we identify individuals who possess the necessary skills and qualities to effectively lead the team?
13. What steps can we take to involve various members of the faith community and prevent overreliance on specific groups or individuals?
14. How can we leverage the influence of known leaders within our church, both those with official titles and those with informal influence?
15. In what ways can their involvement contribute to the success of the evangelization team's initiatives?

# 10

# Catch the Spark

## Taking Revitalization Cues from Growing Parishes

Let the wise also hear and gain in learning,
and the discerning acquire skill.

—Proverbs 1:5

Visiting innovative, thriving churches and parishes is one of the most valuable things a pastor and his team can do when seeking to catalyze growth and revitalization in their own faith community. There's no more effective way to envision what can be achieved than by immersing yourself in a community where the Spirit is actively motivating people to share their faith and deepen their relationship with God. Directly observing what other churches are doing to foster evangelization and vibrant ministries provides tangible ideas, energy and hope for revitalization at home.

When looking for churches or parishes to visit, look for sustained increases in attendance, giving, baptisms, volunteers or other relevant metrics over a five- to ten-year period. The growth should also be spiritual and missional, not just numerical. Search for churches with a reputation for engaging worship, active lay participation, strong evangelization and service to the community. A recommendation from a denominational leader or ministry partner is invaluable. Within driving distance is ideal, but look nationally and internationally for inspiring examples and plan site visits, if needed.

Once a church is selected, reach out to the pastor or staff to schedule a visit. Be upfront about your desire to learn from their revitalization journey. Ask if they are open to hosting your team for a day or two to immerse yourselves in their culture and ministry model. If possible, plan visits to experience a weekend service, observe ministry programs in action and interview church leaders and volunteers. Work with them to tailor an itinerary focused on your specific areas of interest and needs.

To maximize learnings, develop a list of key questions for church leaders ahead of the visit. Ask about the history of their revitalization, biggest "wins," greatest challenges, and how they measure success. Inquire about staff roles, organizational structure, lay mobilization, discipleship systems, evangelization approaches and growth processes. Request copies of strategic plans or ministry calendars to review. During the visit, take notes on ideas and observations that could be applied in your own context. Identify any assumptions challenged. Discuss impressions as a team throughout the experience.

While on-site, look for principles and practices that could be replicated back home. Pay attention to the church's facilities, printed materials and use of technology. Observe hospitality elements, music style, preaching approach and how visitors are welcomed. Notice environmental factors like signage, cleanliness, seating, decor and accessibility. Visit faith formation classrooms, observe childcare areas and speak with volunteers. Get a sense of the spiritual vitality and joy present. Ask about struggles they've faced and how challenges were addressed.

After returning from the visit, document key learnings and insights gained while they're fresh. As a team, debrief the experience and identify three to five ideas to implement in the next six months. Turn this into an action plan, designating leaders, needed resources, next steps and target dates. Schedule follow-up calls with the church to clarify or dig deeper on aspects of their model. Quickly act on the momentum generated before it is lost.

Beyond on-site visits, there are other valuable ways to learn from thriving faith communities:

- Read books, blogs or newsletters from pastors of growing churches. Study their websites.
- Listen to homilies, teachings or podcasts from these community's leaders. Follow them on social media.
- Attend denominational or ministry conferences featuring these churches. Take notes.

The possibilities abound. With eyes open to examples of God's work in other places, the inspiration to cultivate such vitality can take root back home. Our own parish is never too far gone that it cannot experience renewal again. There are models and partners available to guide the way. But action must be taken. Through prayer and the Spirit's guidance, step out to visit where God's transformation is unfolding and return ready to write a new story of life and development.

*

Below are some questions aimed at applying the insights gained in this chapter to your parish community.

1. In what ways can we learn from thriving churches and parishes to catalyze our own transformation?
2. What criteria should we consider when selecting churches or parishes to visit?
3. How can we identify faith communities of a similar size and demographic context that have experienced measurable growth in recent years?
4. How can we ensure that the growth is both numerical and spiritual, reflecting a vibrant and missional community?
5. How can we establish connections with the pastors or staff of the churches we wish to visit?
6. What steps can we take to schedule a visit and express our desire to learn from their revitalization journey?

7. What key questions should we prepare ahead of the visit to maximize our learnings?
8. How can we inquire about their history of revitalization, successes, challenges and how they measure success?
9. During the visit, what specific elements should we pay attention to that could be replicated in our own context?
10. How can we observe and learn from their facilities, hospitality, worship, preaching, discipleship processes and evangelization programs?
11. How can we document and debrief the key learnings and insights gained from the visit?
12. What steps should we take as a team to identify ideas to implement in the next six months and create an action plan?
13. Apart from on-site visits, what other valuable ways can we learn from thriving faith communities? How can we engage with their resources such as books, blogs, newsletters, homilies, teachings, podcasts and social media?
14. How can we maintain the momentum generated from the visit and quickly act on the ideas and inspiration gained?
15. What strategies can we employ to ensure that the learnings are effectively implemented in our own faith community?
16. How can prayer and the guidance of the Holy Spirit inspire and guide us as we step out to visit thriving churches and return to write a new story of life and development in our own parish?

# 11

# Against the Odds
## Revitalizing Rural Parishes

Growth is possible in rural multi-church groups where the right conditions are in place.

–Church of England, *Shaping Strategies for Mission and Growth in Multi-Church Groups*, 2017

Rural parishes face a unique set of challenges that can sometimes make evangelization and vitality seem like insurmountable goals. Declining and aging populations, few resources and maintenance burdens on aging buildings all contribute to a sense of struggle or even despair. However, with intentionality, creativity and a focus on empowering laity, rural parishes can tap into their potential to become strong, missional faith communities.

The core foundation must be a focus on mission and outreach. Rural churches, like other parishes, are very often overly inward-focused on simply maintaining programs or buildings. Shifting this mindset to prioritize evangelization and service is critical. By fostering a missional culture, clergy and lay leaders can equip parishioners to live out their calling to proclaim the word of God.

This begins with training laity in relational evangelization and providing outlets to practise sharing their faith through existing connections in a close-knit rural setting. Outreach initiatives that meet real needs like poverty, loneliness or poor access to health care are also important ways to build connections and demonstrate the real nature of the Church. Rural parishes must find ways to be present and engaged outside church activities.

Lay mobilization and leadership development are essential. Rural faith communities are often small, meaning few people are available to take on roles. Still, leaders should identify and come alongside emerging lay leaders, providing mentorship, training and spiritual formation tailored to their rural context. Equipping laity to lead small groups, provide pastoral care, handle administration or grow in their preaching abilities empowers the entire body of Christ to participate in ministry.

Creativity in worship and discipleship can help connect with diverse rural communities.

Traditional Sunday services certainly have value, but rural churches should also offer gatherings throughout the week, leveraging technology and alternative contexts. Fresh expressions of church that reflect local rural culture are one way to engage dechurched populations. Discipling current members through Bible studies, prayer groups, leadership development and outdoor retreats focused on spiritual growth provides balance.

Unity and shared vision across the multiple faith communities that make up rural multi-parish groups prevents isolation and pools resources. It is important for clergy to maintain individual parish identities while facilitating collaboration, education and relationship-building across the parish. Streamlining legal and administrative structures when possible can free up energy for more vital efforts.

For clergy, establishing networks of peer support and continuing education focused on the opportunities and challenges of rural ministry helps prevent burnout. Monitoring workload and spiritual/emotional health while providing counselling, sabbaticals and professional development creates sustainability. At the diocesan or deanery level, ensuring clergy are trained and resourced for rural contexts is key.

Rather than compete, rural churches should actively partner with other rural organizations and networks. This facilitates sharing creative ideas, volunteers and funds while also raising the church's visibility. Work with rural schools provides very promising opportunities for connecting with youth and children. And ecumenical cooperation can provide spiritual enrichment and maximize limited resources.

Rural areas hold great spiritual harvests that are ready to be gathered. Through divine grace, openness to change, perseverance and prayer, rural parishes can transcend their decline and embrace a new beginning. By tapping into the relational nature of rural areas, thinking creatively and refusing to simply manage decline, clergy and laity can partner with the Holy Spirit to revitalize their mission.

*

Below are some questions aimed at applying the insights gained in this chapter to a rural parish.

1. How have the unique challenges faced by our rural parish impacted the sense of struggle or despair in our own faith community?
2. What are some practical ways we can foster a missional culture in our rural parish?
3. In what ways can we train and support our laity in relational evangelization within the close- knit rural setting?
4. How can we identify and address the real needs of our community to build connections and demonstrate the nature of the Church?
5. What specific mentorship, training and spiritual formation opportunities can we provide for emerging lay leaders?
6. What alternative contexts, fresh expressions of church and discipleship opportunities can we offer to engage both existing and dechurched populations?
7. How can we foster unity and shared vision across multiple faith communities within rural multi-parish groups?
8. In what ways can clergy facilitate collaboration, education and relationship-building while maintaining individual parish identities?

9. What strategies can we implement to prevent burnout among clergy in rural ministry? How can we establish networks of peer support and prioritize clergy well-being?
10. How can we actively partner with other rural organizations and networks instead of competing with them?
11. What opportunities for sharing ideas, volunteers and funds and for raising visibility can we explore?

12

# Cultivating Spiritual Curiosity
## The Art of Pre-Evangelization

"Let your light so shine before others,
so that they may see your good works
and give glory to your Father in heaven."

—Matthew 5:16

Missionary parishes emphasize actions that call for the involvement of the entire parish community. Parishioners are invited to focus on building new relationships, opening channels of communication with the surrounding community and creating an environment conducive to spiritual discussion. This is what is called pre-evangelization: the preliminary step in the process of sharing one's faith with someone. Activities such as connecting with new people, bringing them together, witnessing to the Gospel and inviting people to church activities are all part of pre-evangelization.

Here are some practical suggestions:

- *Pray to meet people*: Pray that God guides you toward meaningful encounters and opens doors for fruitful exchanges. Prayer forms the very foundation of evangelization.
- *Be proactive*: Build new relationships by participating in local community events or volunteer activities. This is a great way to demonstrate God's love. Start conversations and discover common interests or activities you could take part in together.

- *Offer your support*: Be ready to help and support the people you meet. Acts of kindness and service not only incarnate the teachings of Jesus but also build trust and can open the door to conversations about spirituality and faith.
- *Ask open-ended questions*: During your conversations, use questions to encourage dialogue about faith and spirituality. For example, you might ask, "What do you think happens after death?" or "In what ways do you practise your spirituality?" If the opportunity is right, share your personal testimony and explain how your faith has had a positive impact on your life.
- *Pray*: When someone shares their difficulties and suffering with you, it's a great opportunity to show her God's love. Ask her if you can pray for her right now. With her permission, put your hand on her shoulder or hold your arm out over her and turn to God with confident faith, knowing that nothing is impossible for him.
- *Organize small meetings or events*: Invite friends, including the person you want to reach. These can be casual lunches or dinners, game nights or other social activities that introduce them to other members of the Christian community.
- *Share relevant resources*: Consider giving them a New Testament or another faith-based book that matches their interests or concerns. You can give it as a gift or simply mention a book or article you've found inspiring or helpful.
- *Be a good example*: The best way to share your faith is, of course, to live it. Let your actions speak even louder than your words. Show people Christ's love through your whole life: your words, your actions, your attitudes.
- *Extend the invitation*: When you feel comfortable and the time is right, extend an invitation to attend a liturgy or special event at church. Explain clearly why you love your Christian community and why you think it would be beneficial for them to join.

The purpose of pre-evangelization is to demonstrate Christ's love to new people and to create an environment of trust and friendship. It requires patience, since building authentic relationships takes time. It is also important to consider that some people will not be immediately open to discussing faith, and that's okay.

We should initiate conversations about faith but let others determine the pace and level of comfort. Pre-evangelization is aimed at gradually bringing people to feel comfortable talking about spiritual matters while respecting where they are and their beliefs.

*

Below are some questions aimed at applying the insights gained in this chapter to your personal life or your parish community.

1. How can we prioritize prayer activities for the renewal of our parish and the people we seek to reach?
2. In what ways can we actively build new relationships within our local community?
3. How can we participate in community events or volunteer activities to meet new people and foster connections?
4. What practical ways can we offer support to those we meet?
5. What kinds of questions can we pose to initiate meaningful conversations and create space for sharing personal experiences?
6. How can we show God's love by offering to pray for those who share their difficulties and suffering with us?
7. What types of small meetings or events can we organize to introduce new people to the Christian community?
8. How can we create casual and welcoming environments for social interactions?
9. How can we share relevant resources, such as the New Testament or faith-based books, with those we are seeking to reach?
10. How can we choose materials that match their interests or concerns?

11. In what ways can we let our actions speak louder than our words and demonstrate Christ's love through our whole lives?
12. How can we clearly communicate why we love our Christian community and why it would be beneficial for others to join?
13. How can we initiate conversations about faith while allowing others to determine the pace and level of comfort?

13

# The Point of Decision

## Calling for Life Surrender to Christ

If you confess with your lips that Jesus is Lord and
believe in your heart that God raised him from the dead,
you will be saved.
For one believes with the heart and so is justified,
and one confesses with the mouth and so is saved.

—Romans 10:9-10

Effective evangelization entails not just starting conversations about faith and conveying the central message of the Gospel but also helping others make the choice to receive Christ in their lives. This can be done by guiding listeners to say an act of faith prayer, whether it's in the context of small-group discussions, during one-on-one conversations or at the conclusion of a homily.

But first, what is the central message of the Gospel, often referred to as the kerygma? Here are a few essential points:

- God loves us. (Isaiah 43:4; Jeremiah 31:3) "God is love." (1 John 4:8)
- All people have sinned and fall short of God's glory. (Romans 3:23) Our sin separates us from God. (Isaiah 59:2)
- God "desires everyone to be saved and to come to the knowledge of the truth." (1 Timothy 2:4)
- Jesus Christ, the eternal Son of God, became human to reconcile humanity to God and make us adopted children of God. He died on

the cross to pay the penalty for our sins. (1 Peter 2:24) He rose again, conquering sin and death and proving he is the way to eternal life. (Romans 6:9; 1 Corinthians 15:55-57)

- We receive salvation through faith in Jesus Christ. (John 3:16) Salvation is an undeserved gift. In Jesus Christ, all God's truth has been revealed. He is the truth. (Romans 6:23; Titus 3:5-7; John 14:6)
- Christ calls us all to conversion, offering forgiveness for our sins. Even those who have committed the most serious faults can choose to convert and benefit from God's mercy. (1 John 1:9; Luke 5:32; John 8:10-11) Jesus refuses no one and finds joy in forgiving us. (Luke 15:7; Luke 15:11-32)
- To receive salvation, we must repent, call on the name of the Lord and turn away from sin. (Acts 3:19; Acts 2:21) "Repent, and be baptized every one of you in the name of Jesus Christ so that your sins may be forgiven; and you will receive the gift of the Holy Spirit." (Acts 2:38)
- According to the teaching of the Catholic Church, baptism is necessary for salvation, as it is the means by which we enter the new life in Christ and the Church itself. (Mark 16:16)
- Jesus calls us to follow him and become his disciples. (John 8:12; John 10:27; Mark 8:34) To become a disciple of Christ is to enter a path of continuous conversion.

While the message can be adapted to resonate with different cultures, our mission is not only to make the Gospel message known but also to encourage and help people to *respond to it* by verbalizing an act of faith in Jesus the Saviour.

In his book *Evangelization: A Challenge for the Catholic Church* (published in 2020), Fr. Bob Bedard, a Catholic high school teacher and the founder of the Companions of the Cross, defines evangelization as a three-step process:

1. Clearly proclaiming the Gospel, where individuals understand the call to surrender their lives to the Lord.

2. Guiding and encouraging individuals to make a personal, conscious decision to embrace the Gospel, accept Jesus as Lord and receive salvation.
3. Once this decision is made, God's power is unleashed to transform their lives, leading to an authentic spiritual and religious experience.

Bedard challenged people to let God play an active role in their lives and invited them to make a conscious decision to surrender to Christ. He provided them with a prayer of dedication to vocalize this decision:

> Dear Lord, I bow before you as the great God of heaven and earth and the loving Father of us all. Thank you for calling us to an eternal life of joy with you, made possible for us by the death of Jesus your divine Son, whom you have made King and Lord of all creation.
>
> Lord Jesus, I want to follow you completely. I want to turn away from all sinful patterns in my life. Help me to do this. I choose you as the only Lord and Saviour of my life and surrender everything to you—body and soul, mind and will, past, present and future, priorities and plans, and all my possessions.
>
> Deal with me in whatever way you wish. Come, Holy Spirit. Confirm me in my decision. Glory be to the Father, to the Son and to the Holy Spirit. Amen.[9]

It was not until he began to evangelize in this way that he saw his students touched deeply by the Lord. Before that, many of them stopped practising their faith entirely when they left school. They seemed to view their faith as something confined to the school environment, disconnected from their daily lives. But the turning point in their spiritual journeys was the day they made a conscious choice for Jesus and his Gospel.

*

9 This prayer can be found in Fr. Bob Bedard's book *Evangelization: A Challenge for the Catholic Church*. Used with permission from the Companions of the Cross.

Below are some questions aimed at applying the insights gained in this chapter to your personal life or your parish community.

1. How would you summarize the core message of the Gospel, or the kerygma, based on the essential elements mentioned in the text?
2. In what ways can I effectively communicate the Gospel message to others?
3. Which programs, videos or tools can I use to guide individuals toward committing their lives to Christ?
4. What does it mean to respond to the Gospel?
5. How can I help others make a conscious decision to accept Jesus after hearing the Gospel message?
6. How can small groups in our parish better incorporate times for people to verbalize receiving Christ?
7. What practical steps can I take to create opportunities for people to respond to the Gospel within my parish?
8. How might the priest or deacon, from the ambo after a homily, play a role in assisting individuals in welcoming Christ into their lives?

# 14

# Catalyzing Change
## A Comprehensive Approach to Parish Assessment

All organizations, especially churches, will deteriorate if left on their own. A helpful evaluation exercise is to list areas that need improvement. Be specific. Then work on that list as if it were a 'to do' list.

–Dale Galloway, *Making Church Relevant*

To effectively revitalize a parish, it is crucial for priests to develop a deep understanding of their community's current reality. This understanding comes through an honest and realistic assessment of the parish's state, identifying its strengths, weaknesses, opportunities and threats.

The concept of "holy discontent" emerges as a key element in this process of evaluation and renewal. Far from being a negative emotion to be suppressed, this discontent can become a powerful catalyst for positive change when properly channelled. It arises from the tension between the Church's mission to make disciples and the realization that the status quo is often insufficient to meet this call.

This discontent is intimately linked to passion for the Church and its mission. By recognizing areas that are not living up to their potential, priests and engaged laity can develop the motivation necessary to drive meaningful change. However, it is crucial to maintain balance, ensuring that this discontent does not become toxic or turn into cynicism. The goal is to remain anchored in hope and commitment to constructive action.

Parish leaders can use this discontent as a tool to motivate change. By openly addressing the common frustrations of the congregation, they can inspire a collective desire for improvement and pave the way for new ideas and revitalization initiatives.

To structure this evaluation, SWOT analysis (strengths, weaknesses, opportunities, threats) proves to be a valuable tool. This method allows for a systematic analysis of the internal and external factors influencing the health and growth of the parish.

Strengths represent the assets on which the parish can build. These might include a dynamic music program, active prayer groups or a dedicated team of volunteers. Identifying these strengths allows for their effective use to foster growth and maximize the parish's impact in its community.

Weaknesses, on the other hand, are areas that require particular attention and improvement. These may include declining attendance, lack of community engagement or an aging congregation. It is essential to address these weaknesses honestly, without minimizing them, in order to develop ways to overcome them.

Opportunities represent potential avenues for growth and outreach. These might include partnerships with local organizations, initiatives to engage younger generations, or the development of online ministries. By seizing these opportunities, parishes can broaden their reach and increase their impact in the community.

Threats are external factors that could hinder the parish's growth or stability. These may include unfavourable demographic changes, cultural shifts away from traditional religion, or competition from other religious communities. Identifying these threats allows for the development of proactive measures to address them.

Beyond this SWOT analysis, it is important to evaluate several specific aspects of parish life:

**Missionary culture:** This involves examining the extent to which the parish is outward-focused, actively seeking to reach non-believers and make disciples. It requires assessing attitudes, values and behaviours that either promote or hinder missionary momentum within the community.

**Prayer:** An essential aspect of the Church evangelization initiative is prayer. It is important to evaluate the parish's commitment to prayer for its missionary transformation and the people it is trying to reach. This involves assessing the frequency of prayer meetings, the inclusion of evangelization intentions in parish prayers, and the encouragement of personal prayer for missionary efforts. The goal is to ensure that prayer is at the heart of all evangelization efforts, fostering a deep reliance on God's grace and guidance.

**Celebrations:** The evaluation should focus on the quality and impact of liturgical celebrations, including music, accessibility for newcomers and the kerygmatic dimension of homilies. The goal is to ensure that celebrations are both faithful to tradition and relevant to the people we want to reach out to.

**Evangelization:** It is crucial to analyze the parish's efforts to reach those who are not believers. This includes examining strategies to attract newcomers, create welcoming environments and effectively share the Gospel message.

**Discipleship:** The parish's effectiveness in fostering the spiritual growth of its members and equipping them for ministry is an essential aspect. This involves evaluating faith formation programs, participation in small groups, leadership development and spiritual growth opportunities offered to parishioners.

**Fellowship:** The sense of community within the parish is a crucial element of its vitality. The evaluation should focus on opportunities for connection between members, the quality of hospitality and the community's ability to support those in need.

**Ministries:** The effectiveness of various ministries within the parish should be examined. This involves assessing their alignment with the overall mission of the parish, their impact on the community, and their ability to mobilize the gifts and talents of parishioners.

**Planning:** Finally, it is important to evaluate the parish's capacity to develop and implement a long-term action plan. This involves examining decision-making processes, resource management and the alignment of actions with the parish's vision and objectives.

This comprehensive evaluation should be conducted collaboratively, involving parishioners and leadership teams. A collaborative approach allows for diverse perspectives and fosters a shared commitment to the revitalization process.

Once the evaluation is complete, the next step is to develop a pastoral plan that builds on identified strengths, addresses weaknesses, exploits opportunities and mitigates threats. This plan should include specific objectives, concrete actions, realistic timelines and clearly assigned responsibilities.

In conclusion, understanding parish reality and creating a pastoral plan is a demanding but essential process for any priest wishing to lead their community toward authentic renewal. By adopting an honest, structured and collaborative approach, parishes can empower themselves to fully realize their mission in today's world, transforming "holy discontent" into a driving force for positive and lasting change.

*

Below are some questions aimed at applying the insights gained in this chapter to your parish community.

1. How can we identify and constructively channel "holy discontent" in our parish without letting it become toxic or cynical?
2. How committed is our parish to prayer for its missionary transformation, and how can we ensure that prayer remains central to all our evangelization efforts?
3. In conducting a SWOT analysis of our parish, what do you believe are our key strengths and weaknesses? How can we leverage our strengths and address our weaknesses?
4. What opportunities do you see for our parish to grow and expand its impact in the community? Are there any potential threats we should be aware of and prepare for?

5. How would you assess our parish's current missionary culture? What steps can we take to become more outward-focused and actively engaged in making disciples?
6. Reflecting on our liturgical celebrations, how can we ensure they are both faithful to tradition and relevant to the people we want to reach out to? What improvements could be made?
7. What strategies could we implement to more effectively reach the unchurched and create a welcoming environment for newcomers?
8. How well does our parish foster the spiritual growth of its members and equip them for evangelization and ministry? What additional resources or programs might be beneficial?
9. In what ways can we strengthen the sense of fellowship and community within our parish? How can we improve our support for those in need?
10. Considering our various ministries, how well do they align with our overall mission? Are there any gaps or areas where we could be more effective?
11. How can we improve our long-term planning and decision-making processes to better align our actions with our parish's vision and objectives?

15

# From Vision to Action
## Planning for Parish Revitalization

The longer I'm in the ministry, the more I recognize the importance of taking the time for good planning. Nothing happens unless the leaders of a church plan for it to happen. Don't wait for your ship to come in, swim out to it.

—Dale Galloway, *20/20 Vision*

Continuing to build upon the concepts introduced in the previous chapter, this section discusses the practical aspects of planning for parish revitalization. While some key themes will be revisited, we'll expand on these ideas and provide more detailed methods for putting them into action.

**Defining the church's mission and vision:** Revitalizing a dying church or parish is a challenging but essential task that requires careful planning, dedication and a willingness to embrace change. The process begins with defining the church's mission and vision, which serve as the foundation for all revitalization efforts.

A parish mission statement should clearly articulate why it exists. It needs to be concise, measurable and easily communicated to others. The vision statement, on the other hand, paints a picture of the parish's desired future. Both statements should be deeply rooted in Scripture, reflect the church's theological perspective, and take into account its location, context and culture.

When crafting these statements, churches often turn to the Great Commandment (Matthew 22:37-40) and the Great Commission (Matthew 28:19-20) as starting points. These biblical passages provide a solid foundation for defining a church's purpose and aspirations. The mission statement typically focuses on making disciples, while the vision statement describes what the parish hopes to become.

**Sharing the vision:** Effective communication of these statements is key. Church leaders should share the vision frequently and passionately, inspiring members to embrace and work toward it. The vision needs to ignite passion within the congregation and provide a clear direction for the church's future.

**Assessing the church's current state:** Once the mission and vision are established, the next step is to assess the church's current state. This involves conducting a thorough analysis of the parish's strengths, weaknesses, opportunities and threats (SWOT analysis), as introduced in the previous chapter. This evaluation helps identify the starting point for revitalization efforts and highlights areas that require immediate attention.

**Developing a comprehensive plan:** With a clear understanding of the church's mission, vision and current state, the next phase involves developing a comprehensive plan to achieve the desired goals. This plan should be detailed and include specific, measurable, achievable, relevant and time-bound (SMART) objectives.

**Focusing on evangelization and discipleship:** One key aspect of the plan must be a renewed focus on evangelization and discipleship. These should be central priorities guiding all parish activities. Churches grow when they prioritize bringing people to Christ and helping them deepen their faith. Programs like Alpha can be effective tools for introducing newcomers to the Christian faith.

**Creating a discipleship process:** Creating a clear discipleship process is also crucial. This involves developing a structured path that helps individuals grow in their faith, from initial encounter to mature discipleship. While there are models available, each parish should tailor its process to its unique context and needs.

**Building a foundation of prayer:** Prayer should be at the heart of all revitalization efforts. Heartfelt, intercessory prayer is often cited as the single most important ingredient for church renewal. It fuels outreach efforts and keeps the focus on God's will for the church.

**Creating a welcoming environment:** Creating a welcoming environment is another critical aspect of church revitalization. Leaders should *evaluate their parish through the eyes of a newcomer*, considering factors such as accessibility, engagement, music, homilies, and the overall atmosphere. Weekend services should be designed to speak to people who may not be familiar with the faith, while still nurturing long-time members.

**Developing lay leadership:** Developing lay leadership is essential for sustainable church growth. Empowering the laity to share ownership of the church's mission can breathe new life into a parish. One way to do this is by forming an evangelization team comprised of passionate parishioners who can help drive the revitalization efforts.

**Learning from other missionary and growing churches:** Learning from other churches can provide valuable insights and inspiration. Visiting thriving parishes of similar size and demographics can help leaders envision what is possible for their own church. This will spark ideas and strategies that can be adapted to fit their unique context.

**Being open to adapting:** A willingness to change is paramount in the revitalization process. Churches must be open to adapting, innovating and making difficult decisions. This might involve evaluating existing ministries and programs to determine which are essential and which could be pruned or eliminated to free up resources for new initiatives.

**Explaining the proposed changes:** Effective communication is essential throughout the revitalization process. Churches should be mindful of the language they use, avoiding "churchy" jargon that is incomprehensible to those outside the faith. It's important to clearly explain the reasoning behind any proposed changes, particularly when those changes might be unpopular or challenging for some members.

**Creating a timeline:** Creating a realistic timeline is an important part of the planning process. Large goals should be broken down into smaller, manageable steps with specific deadlines. It's important to be realistic about what can be accomplished within a given timeframe to avoid burnout and discouragement.

**Assigning responsibilities:** Assigning responsibilities is another critical aspect of the revitalization plan. Churches often struggle with an imbalance of strengths on their leadership teams, with an overabundance of relational or executing roles and a shortage of functional or influencing gifts. Successful revitalization requires leaders who can not only develop a plan but also inspire others to follow it and delegate tasks effectively.

**Establishing accountability measures:** Establishing accountability measures is essential for tracking progress and ensuring the parish stays focused on its goals. Regular evaluations using tools like a "Church Revitalization Checklist" can help measure progress and identify areas that need attention.

**Communicating the plan:** The revitalization plan should be communicated clearly and consistently to everyone in the parish. Transparency about the plan, timeline and each person's role helps ensure buy-in from the congregation. While resistance to change is normal, effective communication about the reasons behind the changes can help minimize opposition.

**Maintaining flexibility:** Flexibility is a must throughout the revitalization process. Things will inevitably change, and the plan should be regularly reviewed and updated, particularly at key points such as the six-month, one-year and three-year marks. This includes being willing to trim away activities that are no longer serving the church's mission and focusing efforts on initiatives that promote growth.

**Celebrating successes:** Finally, it's important to celebrate successes along the way. Recognizing and commemorating milestones and accomplishments helps maintain momentum and enthusiasm for the revitalization efforts.

In conclusion, revitalizing a dying church requires more than just a list of tasks to complete. It demands a commitment to prayer, a willingness to change and an unwavering focus on the mission of the Church. Patience and persistence are vital, as meaningful change takes time. By following these guidelines and remaining open to God's leading, struggling parishes can find new life and vitality, becoming vibrant centres of faith and community once again.

*

Below are some questions aimed at applying the insights gained in this chapter to your personal life or your parish community.

1. How can we craft mission and vision statements that truly capture our parish's evangelization purpose?
2. In what ways can we more effectively communicate our parish's vision to inspire and engage all members of our congregation?
3. What steps can we take to create a more welcoming environment for newcomers, and how might we evaluate our parish through their eyes?
4. How can we develop a clear discipleship process that guides individuals from their initial encounter with faith to mature discipleship?
5. What role does prayer currently play in our parish's life, and how can we make it more central to our revitalization efforts?
6. How can we better empower and develop lay leadership within our parish? What opportunities exist for increased involvement of passionate parishioners?
7. Are there missionary and growing parishes or churches that we could learn from?
8. How open are we to change as a parish? What areas might require difficult decisions or innovative approaches?
9. How can we improve our communication strategies, especially when explaining the reasons behind proposed changes that might be challenging for some members?
10. What accountability measures could we implement to track our progress and ensure we stay focused on our revitalization goals?

16

# Wherever He Leads

## Following God's Call to Share the Gospel

"I am with you always, to the end of the age."

–Matthew 28:20

Jesus commissioned his followers to "Go and make disciples of all nations" (Matthew 28:19). This call to spread the Gospel and invite people to become followers of Christ remains the essential mission of the Church today. But sharing the Gospel is not always easy. There are times when those we are trying to reach could show indifference, resistance, even hostility. Our efforts to make disciples can also be opposed by negative spiritual forces. As Scripture says, "For our struggle is not against enemies of blood and flesh, but against the rulers, against the authorities, against the cosmic powers of this present darkness, against the spiritual forces of evil in the heavenly places" (Ephesians 6:12).

In the face of opposition, it is tempting to become discouraged and abandon our efforts altogether. However, and despite the obstacles we may encounter, Jesus commissions us to evangelize and make disciples. We wouldn't have been sent if it weren't possible. As his followers, we are called to persevere, no matter how difficult bringing the message of salvation to the world may seem. With God's help and presence, the power of the Gospel will ultimately prevail over human resistance or spiritual attacks.

Observing the early apostles, we see that they boldly kept on preaching Christ. Acts 5:42 says, "And every day in the temple and at home they did not cease to teach and proclaim Jesus as Messiah." When persecution scattered the first Christians from Jerusalem, they went everywhere proclaiming the word of God (Acts 8:4). We, too, must press on consistently, despite any hardships we may face. With God's help, we will bring others to Christ. We may invest much prayer, love and witness into people's lives before seeing any fruit, but the spiritual harvest will come in due time if we do not give up.

This book offers a clear and practical guide for priests and parish councils to transform their parishes into mission-focused communities. It contains all the information needed to develop a pastoral plan with specific actions and strategies.

When using it and moving forward toward revitalization, we believe it is important to avoid language that suggests failure or implies that individuals have done something wrong in the past. Instead, the focus should be on building people up, fostering confidence and empowering them to contribute to the strengthening of their parish. Emphasizing the potential for growth and the positive impact that individuals can have cultivates a sense of purpose and motivation to work together toward a thriving and vibrant community.

Ultimately, a balanced approach that appreciates the existing strengths of a parish while also recognizing areas for growth and improvement will create an environment where individuals feel valued, empowered and motivated to contribute their unique gifts and talents to the journey of revitalization.

The key insights explored in this book can be summarized as follows:

- *Evangelization should be the central priority guiding everything a parish does.* Proclaiming the Good News of salvation through Christ and drawing people into relationship with him is the Church's purpose. When this outward dynamism is missing, parish life stagnates.
- *Heartfelt prayer fuels all fruitful outreach efforts.* Intercession opens hearts to receive the Gospel message. Our human labours bear lasting

fruit only through the Holy Spirit's action in response to prayer. Apart from God, we can do nothing.

- *Building personal relationships and sharing our faith stories with family and friends is highly impactful.* The Gospel message spreads primarily through networks of trusted relationships. Our lived witness gives credibility to our message.
- *Parishes desiring renewal must humbly evaluate themselves and make changes to become more outwardly focused.* This requires recasting vision, training for evangelization and outreach, streamlining programs and potentially pruning less-essential ministries. Change takes sustained effort but is essential for growth.
- *Parishes should strive to provide visitors with a memorable weekend experience.* For most unchurched visitors, weekend celebrations will be their first and most important impression of the Church. Therefore, missionary churches pay very close attention to the weekend experience, striving to make services relevant, accessible and welcoming to newcomers.
- *Communicating the Gospel clearly calls people to believe, respond to God's call and commit their lives to following Jesus Christ.* This response is the foundation for a lifelong journey of faith.
- *Empowering laity for ministry and developing new leaders strengthens parishes over the long term and multiplies impact.* Priests serve as equippers who mobilize and train the body of Christ.
- *Remembering complete dependence on the Holy Spirit is crucial.* Apart from the Holy Spirit, even excellent programs and methods are useless. But empowered by the Spirit, our human efforts gain divine effectiveness. Reliance on the Spirit brings new life.

Jesus desires all people to know his love and experience his salvation. We have the privilege of joining him in fulfilling the Great Commission. Despite challenging times, fields stand ripe for harvest. May this book expand our vision of what is possible. Christ can revitalize parishes and turn them into missionary hubs. Jesus promised that if we abide in him, we will bear much fruit to God's glory.

As we pray persistently and faithfully proclaim the Gospel, our humble efforts will bear fruit. Joy awaits us as we experience the privilege of partnering with God. May Christ's love and Mary's intercession compel us to faithfully steward the sacred calling we have received until more and more people joyfully proclaim, "Worthy is the Lamb who was slain!"[10]

10 Revelation 5:12.

# Bibliography


Bedard, Bob. *Evangelization: A Challenge for the Catholic Church*. Ottawa, ON: Companions of the Cross, 1994.

Church of England. *A Summary of Key Findings and Implications of Recent Research*. London: Church House Publishing, 2004.

Congregation for the Evangelization of Peoples. *Pastoral Guide for Diocesan Priests*. Rome: 1989.

Galloway, Dale. *20/20 Vision: How to Create a Successful Church with Lay Pastors and Cell Groups*. Portland, OR: Scott Publishing Company, 1986.

Galloway, Dale. *Making Church Relevant*. Kansas City, MO: Beacon Hill Press, 1999.

Mallon, James. *Divine Renovation Guidebook: A Step-by-Step Manual for Transforming Your Parish*. Toronto: Novalis, 2016.

Pope Paul VI. *Evangelii Nuntiandi*. Vatican City: Libreria Editrice Vaticana, 1975.

Saint John Paul II. "Homily at the Grant Park in Chicago." October 5, 1979.

Stetzer, Ed, and Mike Dodson. *Comeback Churches: How 300 Churches Turned Around and Yours Can Too*. Nashville, TN: B&H Publishing Group, 2007.

Warren, Rick. *The Purpose Driven Church: Every Church Is Big in God's Eyes*. Grand Rapids, MI: Zondervan, 1995.

White, Rev. Michael, and Tom Corcoran. *Rebuilt: Awakening the Faithful, Reaching the Lost, and Making Church Matter*. Notre Dame, IN: Ave Maria Press, 2013.

# About the Author

Pierre-Alain Giffard is a Canadian theologian, author and educator who is currently serving as the Director of Pastoral Work in the Diocese of Pembroke, Ontario.

He earned a Master of Arts and a Ph.D. in theology from the Université de Montréal, focusing his research on parish revitalization and growth. While primarily involved with various dioceses, Dr. Giffard also held the positions of professor and director of Practical Theology at Saint Paul University in Ottawa. He strongly advocates for the Church's essential role in the world. Driven by a desire to assist churches in the mission of evangelizing and making disciples, he willingly shares his knowledge and experience at conferences and workshops focused on theology and pastoral leadership.

He can be contacted via the following email address:

Email: pierre.alain.giffard@gmail.com

Facebook ID: 100058054550023